EXPLORE THE WORLD

THE GEOGRAPHY OF AUSTRALIA AND THE PACIFIC REALM

SHANNON H. HARTS

PowerKiDS
press.
New York

Published in 2021 by The Rosen Publishing Group, Inc.
29 East 21st Street, New York, NY 10010

First Edition

Editor: Caitie McAneney
Book Design: Tanya Dellaccio

Photo Credits: Cover Norimoto/iStock/Getty Images; p. 4 https://upload.wikimedia.org/wikipedia/commons/a/aa/Pacific_Culture_Areas.png; p. 5 Yunsun_Kim/Shutterstock.com; p. 7 (top) Auscape/Universal Images Group/Getty Images; p. 7 (bottom) TED MEAD/Stone/Getty Images; p. 8 © iStockphoto.com/Rainer Lesniewski; p. 9 (top) Tanya Ann Photography/Moment/Getty Images; p. 9 (bottom) © iStockphoto.com/Nigel Marsh; p. 11 burroblando/iStock/Getty Images; pp. 13, 17 De Agostini Picture Library/Getty Images; p. 15 AsiaTravel/Shutterstock.com; p. 16 Image courtesy of the Earth Science and Remote Sensing Unit, NASA Johnson Space Center; p. 19 JOUAN/RIUS/Gamma-Rapho/Getty Images; p. 20 https://upload.wikimedia.org/wikipedia/commons/5/52/Pacific_Ring_of_Fire.svg; p. 21 AFP/Getty Images; p. 23 Anadolu Agency/Getty Images; p. 25 DEAN TREML/AFP/Getty Images; p. 27 (top) Andrew Merry/Moment/Getty Images; p. 27 (bottom) Yatra/Shutterstock.com; p. 29 James Gourley/Getty Images News/Getty Images.

Cataloging-in-Publication Data
Names: Harts, Shannon H.
Title: The geography of Australia and the Pacific Realm / Shannon H. Harts.
Description: New York : PowerKids Press, 2021. | Series: Explore the world | Includes glossary and index.
Identifiers: ISBN 9781725322202 (pbk.) | ISBN 9781725322226 (library bound) | ISBN 9781725322219 (6 pack) | ISBN 9781725322233 (ebook)
Subjects: LCSH: Australia–Juvenile literature. | Australia–Geography–Juvenile literature. | Oceania–Juvenile literature. | Oceania–Geography–Juvenile literature. | Pacific Area–Geography–Juvenile literature.
Classification: LCC DU96.H38 2021 | DDC 994–dc2

Manufactured in the United States of America

CPSIA Compliance Information: Batch #CSPK20: For Further Information contact Rosen Publishing, New York, New York at 1-800-237-9932

Find us on

CONTENTS

A JOURNEY TO THE PACIFIC 4

AMAZING AUSTRALIA 6

UNDERWATER WONDERS 8

A PEEK AT POLYNESIA 10

NAVIGATING THE OCEAN 12

MELANESIA AND MICRONESIA 14

A COLONIAL PAST 16

REMARKABLE NATURAL RESOURCES 18

LIFE IN THE RING OF FIRE 20

MOUNTAINS AND VOLCANOES 22

SCENIC CITIES 24

CLIMATE ADAPTATIONS 26

WORKING FOR THE FUTURE 28

GLOSSARY 30

FOR MORE INFORMATION 31

INDEX 32

A JOURNEY TO THE PACIFIC

Imagine a region characterized by the huge Pacific Ocean, yet also featuring deserts, volcanos, and forests. It's home to animals and plants that exist nowhere else on Earth, from the koala bear to the duck-billed platypus. This unique region is Australia and the Pacific realm.

The geography of this region is quite **diverse**. The Pacific Islands are a main feature of the Pacific realm region. They include the larger islands of New Zealand and New Guinea as well as thousands of smaller islands. Three major groups of islands in this region are Melanesia, Micronesia, and Polynesia.

Australia is not part of the Pacific realm, but it is often included in a term for the broader region: Oceania. Australia is an island, a country, and a continent.

The Pacific realm encompasses three major culture areas: Polynesia, Melanesia, and Micronesia. Australia lies to the southwest of the realm.

DIVERSE: DIFFERENT OR VARIED.

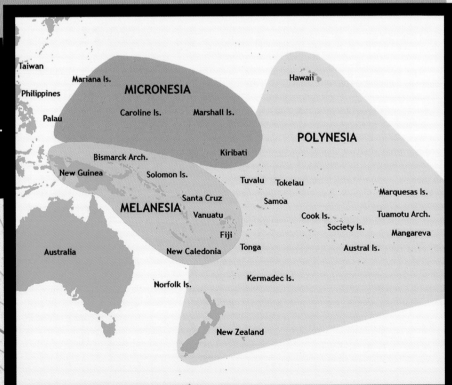

Taiwan
Philippines
Palau
Mariana Is.
MICRONESIA
Caroline Is.
Marshall Is.
Hawaii
POLYNESIA
Bismarck Arch.
New Guinea
Solomon Is.
Kiribati
Tuvalu
Tokelau
Santa Cruz
Samoa
Marquesas Is.
MELANESIA
Vanuatu
Cook Is.
Tuamotu Arch.
Society Is.
Mangareva
Fiji
Australia
New Caledonia
Tonga
Austral Is.
Norfolk Is.
Kermadec Is.
New Zealand

4

THREE TYPES OF ISLANDS

Three types of islands make up Oceania—**continental islands**, high islands, and low islands. Continental islands in the Pacific region include Australia, New Zealand, and New Guinea. They are large islands with diverse geography that includes everything from deserts to mountains. High islands are created through volcanic activity, and have a steep peak in the center. Low islands are made up of **coral** and are usually just around sea level. Sometimes, rings of low islands form **atolls**.

CONTINENTAL ISLAND: AN ISLAND FORMED BY TECTONIC PLATE MOVEMENT THAT CAUSES THE RISING AND FOLDING OF THE OCEAN FLOOR.

Beaches, such as Bondi Beach near Sydney, Australia, are major features of the Pacific realm's geography. Tropical tourism plays an important role in the region.

THINK LIKE A GEOGRAPHER

PARTS OF THE PACIFIC REALM HAVE STRONG AMERICAN INFLUENCES. THE STATE OF HAWAII AND THE TERRITORIES OF GUAM AND AMERICAN SAMOA ARE FOUND WITHIN THE PACIFIC REALM.

ATOLL: A CIRCULAR-SHAPED ISLAND THAT HAS FORMED FROM A CORAL REEF.

5

AMAZING AUSTRALIA

Australia is the largest island in the region, covering 2,969,906 square miles (7,692,021.2 sq km). The continent includes rain forests and farmland, as well as dry desert lands. Expansive forests can be found in Australia's northern tropical regions, east coast subtropical regions, and warm and cool southeast temperate zones.

The Great Dividing Range, a mountain chain, runs along Australia's eastern coast. The mountains are a source of water for Australia's rivers and Australia's main source of inland fresh water—the Great Artesian Basin. Many people settle along the coastline to enjoy its sandy beaches and famous water sports, like surfing.

Australia can also be deadly. It is home to deadly weather events, like bushfires, which can create fire tornados. It is also home to some of the world's deadliest animals, like the box jellyfish, the stonefish, the inland taipan snake, and the saltwater crocodile.

THINK LIKE A GEOGRAPHER

ULURU, ALSO KNOWN AS AYERS ROCK, IS AN ISOLATED MASS OF WEATHERED ROCK IN AUSTRALIA'S SOUTHWESTERN NORTHERN TERRITORY. AT 1,142 FEET (348 M) ABOVE THE DESERT PLAIN, IT'S THE WORLD'S LARGEST **MONOLITH**, AND VERY IMPORTANT TO **ABORIGINAL** PEOPLE.

ABORIGINAL: AN ADJECTIVE THAT DESCRIBES ANYONE FROM AN INDIGENOUS GROUP ANYWHERE IN THE WORLD, OR SPECIFICALLY, A MEMBER OF THE INDIGENOUS ABORIGINAL PEOPLES OF AUSTRALIA.

THE OUTSTANDING OUTBACK

Australia's **outback** is the dry, sparsely populated inland areas of Australia, including the Gibson, Great Sandy, Great Victoria, and Tanami deserts. The Great Victoria Desert is the largest, featuring a vast expanse of sand hills, dry salt lakes, and stony plains in western and southern Australia. The region doesn't receive much rainfall. Some places get fewer than 6 inches [15.2 cm] of rain per year. Extreme temperatures are also common, and **desertification** is a growing concern in Australia.

BEADED GECKO

OUTBACK: THE ARID INLAND AREAS OF THE AUSTRALIAN CONTINENT.

While it doesn't support much human life, the Great Victoria Desert contains many reserves that support a variety of wildlife, including 95 reptile species and 15 bird species. Adaptations allow wildlife to thrive in dry areas.

ADAPTATION: A CHANGE IN A LIVING THING THAT HELPS IT LIVE BETTER IN ITS HABITAT.

UNDERWATER WONDERS

Some of Australia's most vibrant views can only be seen underwater. Australia's famous Great Barrier **Reef** is Earth's largest living structure. It's about the size of Finland, covering nearly 135,000 square miles (349,648.4 sq km). It runs in a northwest-to-southeast direction off Australia's northeastern coast in the Coral Sea, which meets the Tasman Sea in the south.

The Great Barrier Reef is made up of 2,100 individual reefs and 800 **fringing reefs**. More than 1,500 species of fish, 400 species of coral, 4,000 species of **mollusks**, and 240 bird species depend on the reef as their habitat. Seven species of sea turtle live in the Great Barrier Reef, including green turtles and loggerhead turtles. Many of these species are endangered, or at risk of dying out.

This map shows the average coral loss in different sections of the Great Barrier Reef.

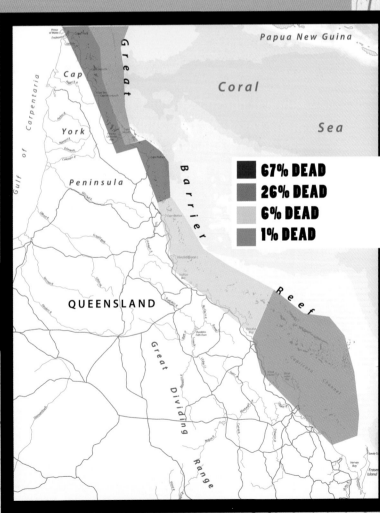

■	**67% DEAD**
■	**26% DEAD**
■	**6% DEAD**
■	**1% DEAD**

REEF: A CHAIN OF ROCKS OR CORAL, OR A RIDGE OF SAND, AT OR NEAR THE WATER'S SURFACE.

THINK LIKE A GEOGRAPHER

THE GREAT BARRIER REEF GENERATES $1.5 BILLION ANNUALLY FOR AUSTRALIA'S ECONOMY THROUGH FISHING AND TOURISM. TOURISM IN AUSTRALIA, THE PACIFIC REALM, AND AROUND THE WORLD WAS HIT HARD BY THE COVID-19 GLOBAL PANDEMIC, WHICH BEGAN IN LATE 2019, AND QUICKLY SPREAD THROUGH TRAVEL AND TRADE.

REEFS FACE RISKS

Climate change makes ocean waters warmer and more acidic, which makes it more difficult for corals to complete the important natural process of calcification, or hardening. Warmer temperatures also block photosynthesis for the algae that provides coral polyps with their bright colors and food. When coral splits from these algae, it becomes stark white in a process called coral bleaching. Eventually, the coral starves to death. Coral bleaching has increased five-fold since 1980 due to climate change.

A PEEK AT POLYNESIA

Melanesia, Micronesia, and Polynesia are the three major island groupings that can be found in the Pacific Islands. Polynesia is a huge area of around 800,000 square miles (2,071,990.5 sq km), with islands in a loose imaginary triangle shape. The points of the triangle are Hawaii, New Zealand, and Easter Island. In between are the islands of Tonga, Tuvalu, and Samoa, among more than 1,000 others. These islands are separated by wide areas of ocean.

Around 4000 BC, Southeast Asian sailors made daring journeys out into the Pacific Ocean, eventually finding Polynesia. The newcomers had to adapt to the hilly, forested islands. They brought plants and domesticated animals to islands that didn't have enough resources to support settlements. They tamed the region's many rugged, steep slopes using a practice called **terrace farming**.

THINK LIKE A GEOGRAPHER

EASTER ISLAND IS IN THE SOUTHEASTERN PART OF THE POLYNESIAN TRIANGLE, A PART OF THE COUNTRY OF CHILE. IT IS KNOWN FOR HUGE ANCIENT STATUES, CALLED *MOAI*.

TERRACE FARMING: A METHOD OF FARMING WHERE FLAT STEPS ARE BUILT INTO THE SIDE OF A HILL OR MOUNTAIN TO CONTROL THE FLOW OF WATER.

NEW ZEALAND

New Zealand is a country made of rugged, mountain-rich islands. Its two major islands—North Island and South Island—are connected by the Cook Strait. The tallest mountain in the country is called Mount Cook. The **indigenous** people of the region, called Maori, refer to the majestic mountain as the "Cloud Piercer." It is just one of many mountains and volcanoes in this island nation. New Zealand is home to more species of flightless birds, including kiwi birds, than any other place in the world. Many are now endangered.

The beautiful, rugged landscape of New Zealand inspired wonder as the backdrop of the popular *Lord of the Rings* movie series.

INDIGENOUS: DESCRIBING GROUPS THAT ARE NATIVE TO A PARTICULAR REGION.

11

NAVIGATING THE OCEAN

The largest feature of this region is not the land itself, but the ocean between islands. The first settlers of Polynesia formed a unique and ocean-centric culture. The first people arrived in today's New Guinea more than 40,000 years ago. Later, around 1600 BC, more arrived from Southeast Asia.

Polynesians became masters of traveling by sea. Ancient Polynesians would travel between the region's many islands using outrigger canoes, which are thin, long boats. They voyaged as far as today's Chile, on the mainland of South America, which is more than 2,000 miles (3,218.7 km) from the closest Polynesian island, Easter Island. Polynesian sea navigators created advanced ways of finding their way between the islands using aspects of nature such as the stars, bird flight patterns, and ocean waves.

THINK LIKE A GEOGRAPHER

POLYNESIAN ISLANDS ARE SEPARATED BY THOUSANDS OF MILES AND DEVELOPED MANY UNIQUE CULTURES OVER TIME. TODAY, MANY NATIVE POLYNESIANS ARE WORKING TO MAINTAIN TRADITIONAL CULTURES AND LANGUAGES.

This engraving shows how ancient Polynesian peoples of the Marquesas Islands navigated using specialized boats.

MASTER MODIFIERS

The Pacific Islands weren't always easy to inhabit. Set apart from other islands, without established crops, they presented many challenges to ancient peoples. However, Polynesians developed **modifications** to survive in their unique environment. Polynesians established successful agriculture on many barren islands by transporting plants and animals by boat. Many people settled near the coast and freshwater sources and learned how to irrigate, or water, the land. They grew crops such as yams, a vegetable called taro, breadfruit, bananas, sugarcane, coconuts, and Tahitian chestnuts.

MODIFICATION: THE PROCESS OF CHANGING THE ENVIRONMENT.

MELANESIA AND MICRONESIA

Melanesia includes an arc of islands north and east of Australia and south of the equator. The area includes the islands of Fiji, the Solomon Islands, the Bismarck **Archipelago**, Vanuatu (formerly the New Hebrides), and New Caledonia. These smaller island countries contain chains of islands, reefs, and archipelagos.

New Guinea is part of Melanesia, and it is the second-largest island in the world. Covered in tropical forests, New Guinea is rich in **biodiversity**. It's home to hundreds of thousands of native species of wildlife, as well as many indigenous tribes of people.

The term "Micronesia" describes both the Federated States of Micronesia and the general geographic area comprising the Mariana Islands, Marshall Islands, Caroline Islands, and Kiribati. The Federated States of Micronesia include the four states of Chuuk, Kosrae, Pohnpei, and Yap.

THINK LIKE A GEOGRAPHER

WAKE ISLAND, GUAM, AND THE NORTHERN MARIANA ISLANDS (INCLUDING SAIPAN) ARE U.S. TERRITORIES.

ARCHIPELAGO: A GROUP OF ISLANDS.

Vanuatu includes about 13 main islands and many smaller ones that run north to south for about 400 miles (643.7 km). Port Vila, pictured here, is the capital city.

TSUNAMIS

Tsunamis are a threat to island countries in the Pacific Ocean. Caused by earthquakes along the ocean floor, tsunamis are huge waves that can seriously harm coastal settlements in the Pacific Islands. Tsunami waves are nearly unnoticeable in the ocean, but they grow as they approach **continental shelves**. Islands like Fiji are often on tsunami watch after Pacific earthquakes, though deadly tsunamis are rare in the region. In 1953, a tsunami hit Suva, the capital of Fiji, causing several deaths and damage to **infrastructure**.

CONTINENTAL SHELF: A PORTION OF A CONTINENT THAT IS SUBMERGED UNDER THE OCEAN AND GRADUALLY SLOPES AWAY FROM THE CONTINENT.

15

A COLONIAL PAST

In 1520, Portuguese explorer Ferdinand Magellan was one of the first Europeans to discover part of Polynesia. While sailing in the Philippines, he spotted the Pukapuka Atoll of the Tuamotu archipelago.

Many other European explorers then followed with an intense desire to spread their Christian faith, increase trading opportunities, and build national pride. The major colonial powers in the region soon became England, France, Spain, and Germany. English became the dominant, or main, language across the region, and many islands today—especially Australia, New Zealand, and New Caledonia—have strong European cultures.

Europeans initially clashed with the indigenous people because European settlers usually didn't give them a say in the governments and trade systems colonists created. To Europeans, Australia and the Pacific realm were *terra nullius*, or "no-man's land."

TUAMOTU ARCHIPELAGO

THINK LIKE A GEOGRAPHER

ABORIGINAL PEOPLES IN AUSTRALIA WERE TRADITIONALLY **NOMADIC**. AFTER EUROPEANS ARRIVED, THOUSANDS OF ABORIGINES DIED FROM DISEASE AND VIOLENCE, AND MANY WERE CONVERTED TO CHRISTIANITY AGAINST THEIR WILL.

PUNISHMENT IN AUSTRALIA

In the late 1700s and early 1800s, Australia was a penal colony, or a place where criminals were sent as punishment. Around 50,000 convicts from England, Ireland, Scotland, and Wales were transported to Australia instead of getting the death penalty. Unfortunately, about a quarter of them didn't survive the long trip to the Pacific island. Many people, including children, were sent to Australia for minor crimes, or simply for being too poor. Colonization of Australia led to cruel violence against aboriginal peoples.

This 1836 engraving shows Matavai Bay in Tahiti being transferred to French missionaries. This is just one example of the ways European colonization took over the Pacific region.

17

REMARKABLE NATURAL RESOURCES

From lush forests to valuable minerals, Australia and the Pacific realm have many remarkable natural resources. The types of natural resources depend greatly on natural landscapes and **biomes**.

Australia is the world's largest producer and exporter, or seller, of the precious stone opal, which is one of many important minerals found throughout Oceania. Iron ore, nickel, gold, diamonds, and zinc are also mined in Australia. The island nation is also the world's largest coal exporter.

The Pacific Islands are large exporters of palm oil, coconut oil, cocoa, coffee, and vanilla. Their forests provide timber and their waters provide ample fishing. The problem with many natural resources in the Pacific Islands comes from overuse. Overfishing and **deforestation** are major issues that show how people can impact the geography of a place negatively.

THINK LIKE A GEOGRAPHER

MANY PACIFIC ISLANDS ARE COVERED IN FORESTS, WHICH ARE A MAJOR SOURCE OF TIMBER. HOWEVER, DEFORESTATION IS THREATENING THE NATURAL LANDSCAPE IN MANY AREAS, INCLUDING THE SOLOMON ISLANDS.

BIOME: A NATURAL COMMUNITY OF PLANTS AND ANIMALS, SUCH AS A FOREST OR DESERT.

Mining for sand in Australia has been shown to cause coastal erosion, or the washing away of sand from valuable beaches on the continental island's coasts.

HYDROPOWER IN NEW ZEALAND

New Zealand's natural resources include coal, limestone, silver, gold, iron ore, and natural gas. However, the country's mining industry is shifting to more minerals for clean technology, such as cobalt and lithium, used in batteries that store renewable energy. Hydropower, which uses dams and machines to create power from moving water, is an important form of renewable energy in New Zealand and other areas of Oceania. In fact, four of the world's top hydropower-producing companies are in the Oceania and Asian regions.

LIFE IN THE RING OF FIRE

Many of the strongest and most deadly earthquakes in history have happened in the **Ring of Fire**. This horseshoe-shaped region extends about 24,900 miles (40,072.7 km) along the boundaries of several **tectonic plates**. When tectonic plates collide, mountains and volcanoes form. When tectonic plates drift apart, deep trenches form. When the plates rub or press against one other and then release energy, earthquakes happen. Because so many plates come together in the Ring of Fire, the region has become home to about 75 percent of Earth's volcanoes and 90 percent of its earthquakes.

Also called the Circum-Pacific Belt, the Ring of Fire includes the Indonesian archipelago, the Philippines, Japan, the Aleutians, the Kuril Islands, Tonga, and Vanuatu. It also includes the North American West Coast and the South American Andes Mountains.

RING OF FIRE: AN AREA WHERE LARGE NUMBERS OF EARTHQUAKES AND VOLCANIC ERUPTIONS OCCUR IN THE BASIN OF THE PACIFIC OCEAN.

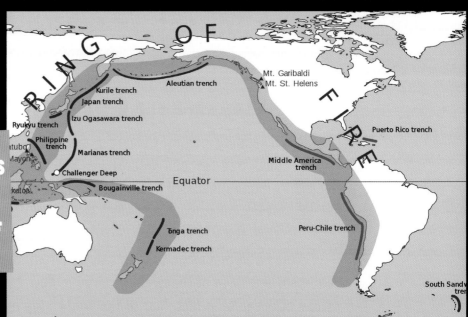

THE WORLD'S MIGHTIEST EARTHQUAKE

On May 22, 1960, the strongest earthquake in history struck 100 miles [160.9 km] off Chile's coast. Like many other ocean earthquakes, it triggered a tsunami. This tsunami didn't just impact Chile; the main island of Hawaii, about 6,200 miles [9,977.9 km] away, also experienced deadly waves around 35 feet [10.7 m] high. The tsunami killed more than 60 people in Hawaii and caused around $75 million in property loss.

An 8.0-**magnitude** earthquake hit the ocean near American Samoa in 2009, causing a tsunami. The earthquake and tsunami killed around 180 people and leveled coastal areas.

THINK LIKE A GEOGRAPHER

ADAPTING TO EARTHQUAKES IS OFTEN MUCH HARDER FOR DEVELOPING COUNTRIES THAT LACK FINANCIAL RESOURCES. EARTHQUAKES CAN DISPLACE PEOPLE FROM THEIR HOMES AND INTERRUPT ECONOMIES FOR YEARS IN HARD-HIT ISLAND NATIONS.

MOUNTAINS AND VOLCANOES

Australia and the Pacific Islands are very mountainous regions because of their location along tectonic plates. Many people think that Mount Everest is the tallest mountain in the world, but that's only if you're measuring from sea level to peak. The tallest mountain from base to peak is actually Mauna Kea in Hawaii. From its start at the ocean floor, Mauna Kea rises up 33,497 feet (10,209.9 m) to its peak. Other high peaks in the region of Oceania include Puncak Jaya in Papua, New Guinea, Mount Cook in New Zealand, and Mount Kosciuszko in Australia.

Mauna Kea is also a **dormant** volcano that hasn't had a serious eruption in about 4,500 years. Active volcanoes in the region include Mauna Loa in Hawaii, Aoba in Vanuatu, Tinakula in the Solomon Islands, and Ulawun in Papua, New Guinea.

DORMANT: IN AN INACTIVE STATE.

THINK LIKE A GEOGRAPHER

SOUTHEAST OF THE MARIANA ISLANDS IN MICRONESIA LIES THE MARIANA TRENCH—THE DEEPEST TRENCH ON EARTH. LIKE MOUNTAINS AND VOLCANOES, TRENCHES ARE CAUSED BY TECTONIC PLATE MOVEMENT.

MOUNT KILAUEA ERUPTION

Hawaii is located on a "hot spot," an area of the seafloor where **magma** erupts, and has many active volcanoes. One vent on Mount Kilauea has been erupting since 1983, but it was mostly under control. Then, in 2018, magma surged from the vent, and red-hot lava flowed toward people's homes. The volcano also let out strands of volcanic glass, plumes of ash, and toxic fumes. The eruption lasted more than four months, damaging 700 structures and costing more than $500 million in damage.

Mount Kilauea erupted in May 2018, damaging structures with its lava flows and sending toxic steam into the air.

SCENIC CITIES

The coastlines of the Pacific realm offer awesome ocean views, peaceful vacation spots, and even bustling cities. Auckland is one of the largest cities in the Pacific realm, located on New Zealand's North Island. It's home to the country's largest port, Waitemata Harbor—an important part of the country's shipping and transportation—along with many roads and railways.

Australia is one of the world's most urban countries. Nearly 90 percent of its residents live in cities. Australia's most populous city is Sydney, the state capital of New South Wales. It's home to the famous Sydney Opera House, Darling Harbor, Bondi Beach, and the Sydney Harbor Bridge. More than 5 million people live in this incredibly **multicultural** city. Melbourne in the state of Victoria and Brisbane in the state of Queensland are also major Australian cities.

THINK LIKE A GEOGRAPHER

HONOLULU, THE CAPITAL CITY OF HAWAII, IS FAR FROM ANY CONTINENTAL MAINLAND, MAKING IT THE MOST REMOTE MAJOR CITY IN THE WORLD.

MULTICULTURAL: HAVING MANY DIFFERENT CULTURES, OR WAYS OF LIFE OF DIFFERENT PEOPLES, IN A UNIFIED SOCIETY.

Auckland is also known for hosting many sailboat races, including races for the America's Cup—one of the oldest and most famous trophies in competitive international sailing.

THE POSSIBILITIES OF PERTH

Perth is Australia's fourth most populous city, and it's on the rise. Like other cities in the region, the variety of economic opportunities has attracted a growing population. Some of the world's largest energy companies are based in Perth. It's an important industrial center for a variety of materials including steel, aluminum, nickel, rubber, cement, and metals. Perth is also home to many universities, parks, art galleries, and cultural centers.

CLIMATE ADAPTATIONS

The mild tropical climate in Australia and the Pacific realm has attracted people for thousands of years. Today, it attracts visitors from all over the world. The climate has also influenced native culture. For example, in the French Polynesian island of Tahiti, traditional clothing was made from light leaves and barks to keep cool in the tropical weather.

Today, new climate challenges are popping up, and people have to adapt. Due to human activity, Earth's **ozone** over Australia has thinned. It cannot block as much **ultraviolet radiation**, which causes sunburn and skin cancer. Australia has one of the highest rates of skin cancer worldwide. In New Zealand and Australia, public campaigns encourage people to "slip" on a T-shirt, "slop" on some sunscreen, and "slap" on a hat for sun protection.

OZONE: THE GASEOUS LAYER AROUND THE EARTH'S ATMOSPHERE THAT BLOCKS HARMFUL RAYS FROM THE SUN.

THINK LIKE A GEOGRAPHER

THE U.N. CLIMATE PANEL SAYS SOME PACIFIC ISLAND NATIONS COULD BECOME "UNINHABITABLE" BECAUSE OF STORMS AND FLOODS DUE TO CLIMATE CHANGE.

BUSHFIRES IN AUSTRALIA

Due to its dry climate, scientists say climate change is fueling more intense bushfires in Australia. In 2019, bushfires burned 7.4 million acres [3 million ha] of land in New South Wales, Australia, between July and December. The fires threatened millions of animals, including native koala bears and other species found only in this region. Mass **evacuations** forced residents from their homes. Firefighters tried to fight against the blaze as it worsened. If the climate in New South Wales continues to be this dry and hot, bushfire seasons will be longer and more deadly.

Australia's climate supports the growth of eucalyptus trees, which are home to koala bears. Rising temperatures could threaten eucalyptus forests and their residents.

WORKING FOR THE FUTURE

Climate change has the power to impact Australia and the Pacific realm forever if it's not kept in check. Rising temperatures threaten native species of plants and animals, pollution and erosion from mining harm the landscape and waterways, and sea levels can rise on already low-lying islands. Without intervention, tragic events like the 2019 Australian bushfires can ruin the unique and beautiful ecosystems of the region.

Fortunately, Australia and most Pacific Island nations signed the Paris Climate Agreement, a worldwide promise to combat and adjust to climate change. Many more challenges likely lie ahead for residents of Australia and the Pacific realm. However, the people of this region will continue to creatively adapt and work to preserve this incredible landscape for future generations.

ADAPTING TO RISING SEAS

Climate change is melting the world's ice sheets, which causes sea levels to rise worldwide—especially in the Pacific realm. As of 2016, at least five reef islands that are part of the Solomon Islands had been lost to sea level rise and coastal erosion. Several communities have had to relocate to avoid being flooded. Many island countries are retracing history by moving from lands settled by European missionaries in the 1900s back to traditional inland native territories.

THINK LIKE A GEOGRAPHER

BARRIER ISLANDS PROVIDE IMPORTANT PROTECTION FROM STORMS THAT COULD DAMAGE COASTS IN OCEANIA. SOME ALSO SUPPORT LARGE POPULATIONS. HOWEVER, THESE ISLANDS ARE PARTICULARLY AT RISK WHEN SEA LEVELS RISE.

BARRIER ISLANDS: ISLANDS FORMED BY SAND DEPOSITED BY SEA CURRENTS ON THE CONTINENTAL SHELF.

The deadly Australian bushfires at the end of 2019 led many residents, especially young people, to protest for government action to address climate change.

GLOSSARY

biodiversity: The number of different types of living things that are found in a certain place on Earth.

coral: A hard skeletal remain produced by a sea creature called a polyp.

deforestation: Clearing forests to use the area for other purposes.

desertification: The process where fertile land turns into desert, usually caused by overgrazing.

evacuation: The act of leaving an area because of danger.

fringing reef: A coral reef that forms near islands or surrounding coastlines.

infrastructure: The equipment and structures needed for a country, state, or region to function properly.

magma: Hot, liquid rock inside Earth.

magnitude: A measure of the power of an earthquake.

mollusk: An animal that lacks a backbone and has a soft body, such as a snail, clam, or octopus.

monolith: A large stone landmass often shaped like a column or pillar.

nomadic: Having to do with people who move from place to place.

tectonic plate: One of the movable masses of rock that create Earth's surface.

ultraviolet radiation: Radiation with wavelengths outside the spectrum of visible light, just beyond violet.

FOR MORE INFORMATION

BOOKS

Medina, Nico. *Where Is the Great Barrier Reef?* New York, NY: Penguin Workshop, 2016.

Somervill, Barbara A. *Australia and Oceania.* New York, NY: Scholastic Children's Press, 2019.

Stine, Megan. *Where Is Easter Island?* New York, NY: Penguin Workshop: New York, NY, 2017.

WEBSITES

All About New Zealand

easyscienceforkids.com/all-about-new-zealand/
Find out more information about New Zealand and what it means to be a Kiwi!

Australia

kids.nationalgeographic.com/explore/countries/australia/
Learn more interesting facts about Australia with National Geographic Kids.

List of Islands in the Pacific Ocean

kids.kiddle.co/List_of_islands_in_the_Pacific_Ocean
Explore this helpful list of the islands in the Pacific Ocean.

INDEX

A

adaptations, 7, 10, 12, 13, 21, 26, 28

animals, 4, 5, 6, 7, 8, 9, 10, 11, 12, 13, 18, 27, 28

C

cities, 5, 15, 24, 25

climate, 6, 7, 9, 26, 27, 28, 29

crops, 13

D

deserts, 4, 5, 6, 7

E

explorers, 16

G

Great Barrier Reef, 8, 9

Great Victoria Desert, 7

I

islands, 4, 5, 6, 10, 11, 12, 13, 14, 15, 17, 18, 20, 21, 22, 24, 26, 28

M

Maori, 11

Melanesia, 10, 14

Micronesia, 10, 14, 22

mountains, 5, 6, 11, 20, 22

N

natural disasters, 6, 15, 20, 21, 22, 23, 26, 27, 29

New Guinea, 4, 5, 12

New Zealand, 4, 5, 10, 11, 16, 19, 22, 24, 26

O

ocean, 4, 5, 10, 12, 15, 21, 22, 24

Oceania, 4, 5, 19, 22, 29

outback, 7

P

plants, 4, 6, 9, 10, 13, 14, 16, 18, 26, 27, 28

Polynesia, 4, 10, 12, 13, 16

R

reefs, 8, 14, 28

resources, 18, 19, 25

Ring of Fire, 20

S

settlers, 10, 12, 16

U

Uluru, 6